HOW YOU CAN SEE HALLEY'S COMET ?

Experts say that you should be able to see Halley's Comet starting in late December, 1985—but you'll probably need binoculars or a telescope. The best time to watch will be in the early evening hours, in the southwest part of the sky.

The comet will be visible, on and off, for the next few months after December. It will be at its brightest from late March to late April, 1986, then it will disappear until the year 2062.

The Comet and You

Written by E.C. KRUPP
Illustrated by ROBIN RECTOR KRUPP

Macmillan Publishing Company
New York

Collier Macmillan Publishers
London

This book is a presentation of Weekly Reader Books.
Weekly Reader Books offers book clubs for children from
preschool through high school.

For further information write to:
Weekly Reader Books
4343 Equity Drive
Columbus, Ohio 43228

Macmillan Publishing Company
866 Third Avenue, New York, N.Y. 10022
Collier Macmillan Canada, Inc.
Printed in the United States of America
10 9 8 7 6 5 4 3 2 1
Library of Congress Cataloging in Publication Data
Krupp, E. C. (Edwin C.), date.
   The comet and you.
   Summary: Presents the history, appearance, and
physical composition of Halley's comet and compares it
to other comets, describing its path through the solar
system and its predicted return.
   1. Halley's comet–Juvenile literature. [1. Halley's
comet.   2. Comets]   I. Krupp, Robin Rector, ill.
II. Title.
QB723.H2K78 1985   523.6′4   84-20152
ISBN 0-02-751250-9

For Margaret and Robert Rector—
whose flamboyance and dependability
are a match for any comet.
R. R. K. and E. C. K.

Comets are found in outer space. Sometimes we see them at night, with the stars. Have you ever seen one? Lots of people have seen Halley's Comet. It's the most famous comet of all.

Like all comets, Halley's is made of three things: ice, gas, and dust. The center, or nucleus, of the comet is solid and much, much smaller than the comet's head.

Tail

Ice

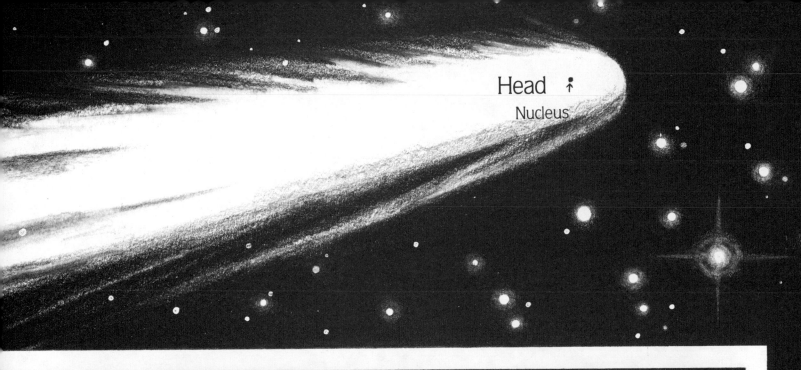

Head

Nucleus

Gas + Dust = A comet

The comet's nucleus is probably a lot like a giant, dirty ice cube. And just as an ice cube steams up in a hot pan, the nucleus forms a fuzzy head of steam and a gassy, dusty tail each time it comes by the sun.

The sun is the center of our neighborhood in space. It is really a star, and we travel around it on the earth.

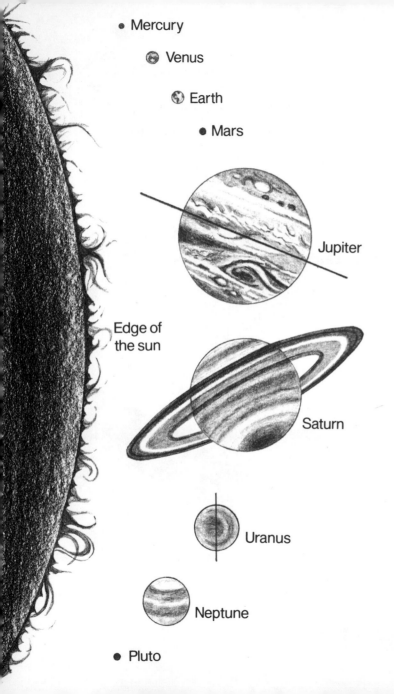

- Mercury
- Venus
- Earth
- Mars

Jupiter

Edge of
the sun

Saturn

Uranus

Neptune

- Pluto

The earth is a planet, and there are nine planets in the sun's family, or solar system.

The planets do not give off their own light. Instead, by reflecting the light of the sun, they shine like mirrors in the nighttime sky. And the planets are much smaller than the sun. If the sun were a basketball, all of the planets put together would be a golfball.

The planets are named Mercury, Venus, Earth, Mars, Jupiter, Saturn, Uranus, Neptune, and Pluto. They circle the sun in paths called orbits, and they are held in their orbits by the force of gravity. The time it takes to get around the sun is different for each planet. The earth completes one orbit in a year, or about 365 days. Comets have orbits, too.

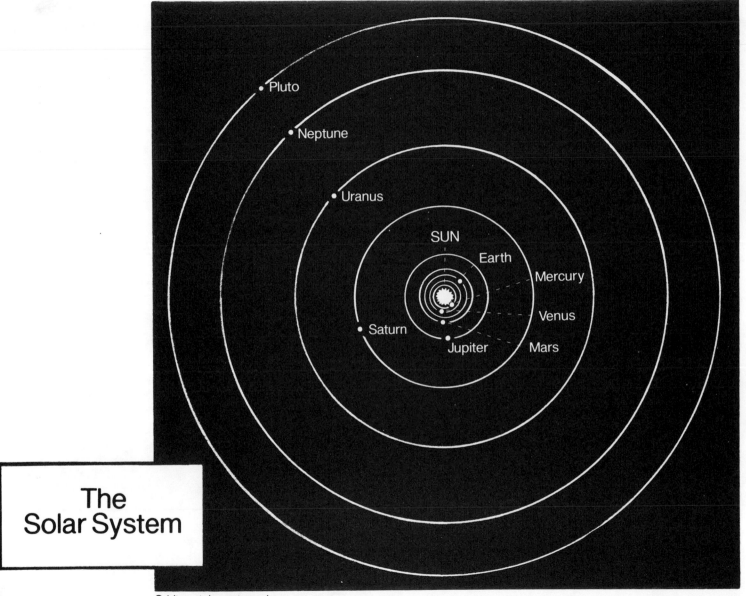

The
Solar System

Orbits not drawn to scale

The mailman comes by almost every day. Your birthday comes by once a year. Halley's Comet comes by every 76 years. That's a long time to wait.

What takes Halley's Comet so long to return? It has a long way to go. Its orbit takes it out beyond the planet Neptune, almost as far as Pluto, the farthest planet.

Some comets return much sooner. Encke's Comet has a small orbit, and so it swings by the sun about once every three years and four months. Other comets don't come back for thousands—even millions—of years. Their orbits are huge.

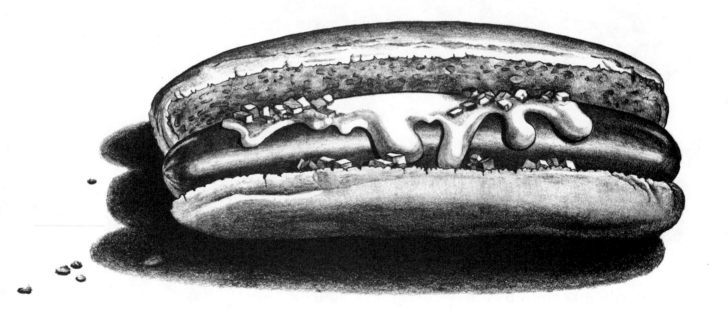

Although the orbits of the planets are almost perfect circles, most comet orbits are long, narrow loops. The path of Halley's Comet is so long and narrow that it looks like a hot dog.

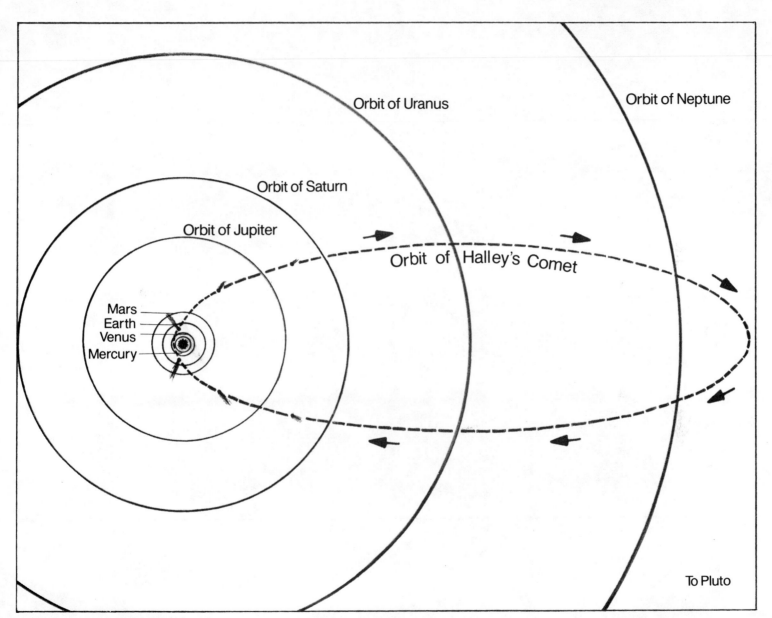

Orbit of Uranus

Orbit of Neptune

Orbit of Saturn

Orbit of Jupiter

Orbit of Halley's Comet

Mars
Earth
Venus
Mercury

To Pluto

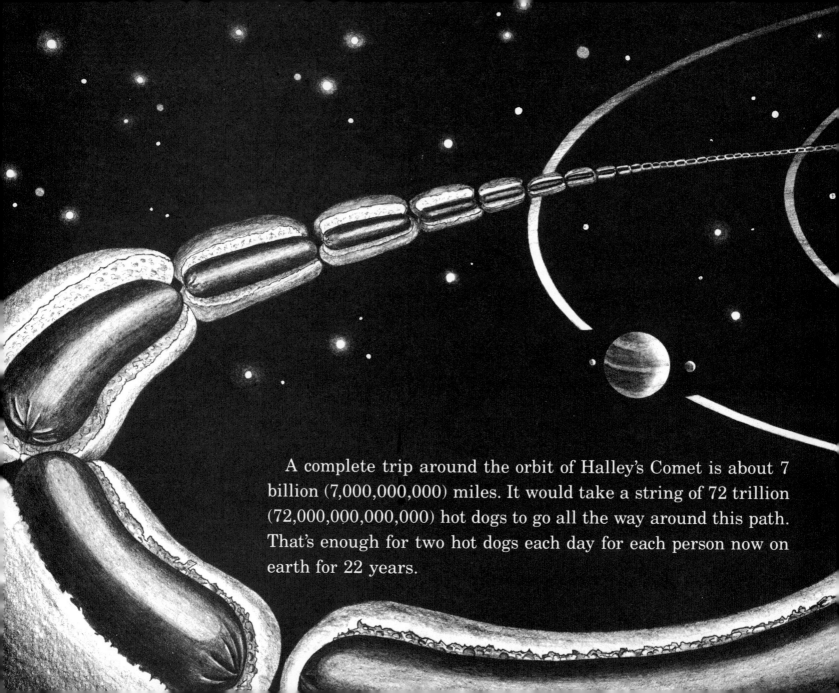

A complete trip around the orbit of Halley's Comet is about 7 billion (7,000,000,000) miles. It would take a string of 72 trillion (72,000,000,000,000) hot dogs to go all the way around this path. That's enough for two hot dogs each day for each person now on earth for 22 years.

Comets are special because we don't see them very often. Most of them seem to show up without warning. And even when one does come by, it doesn't stay around. It's like a friend who comes from the other side of the world to see you and then doesn't even stop to knock on the door.

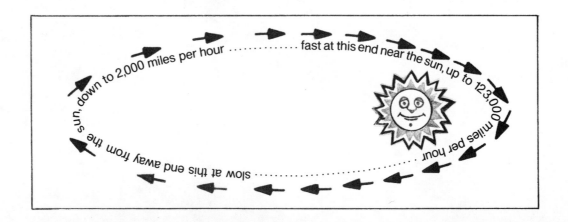

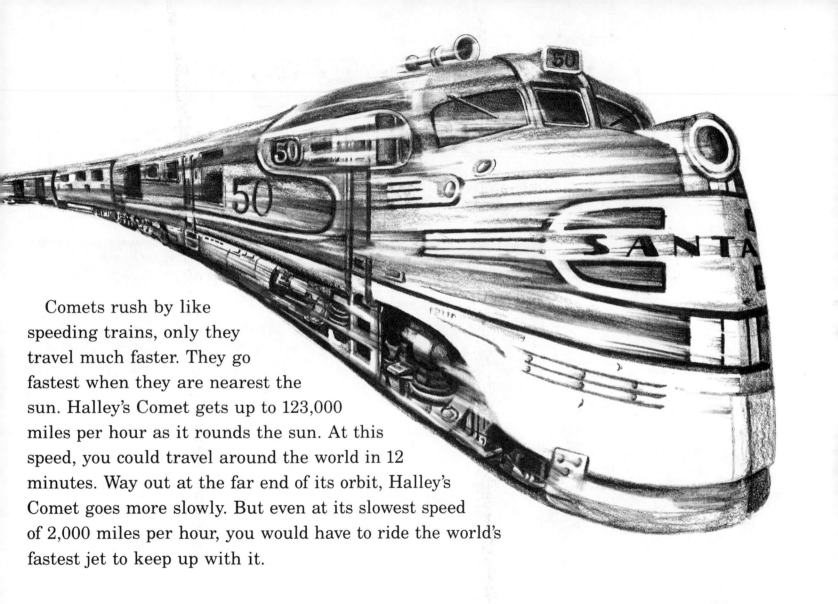

Comets rush by like
speeding trains, only they
travel much faster. They go
fastest when they are nearest the
sun. Halley's Comet gets up to 123,000
miles per hour as it rounds the sun. At this
speed, you could travel around the world in 12
minutes. Way out at the far end of its orbit, Halley's
Comet goes more slowly. But even at its slowest speed
of 2,000 miles per hour, you would have to ride the world's
fastest jet to keep up with it.

The sun appears to rise and set each day, but it is not the sun that's really moving. It is the earth that moves, spinning around like a top. When we are facing the sun, we say that it is "up." When the sun is up, its light is too strong for the stars.

Stars are there in the daytime sky, but they are too faint for us to see. When the turning earth carries us around to face away from the sun, the sky grows dark. And at night, without the light of the sun, we can see the stars rise and set.

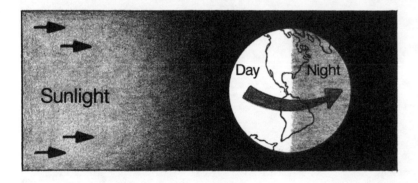

Comets are also hard to see in the daytime, but they show up better at night. And even though a comet moves fast through space, it doesn't just streak through the sky. You will see it night after night. When it is in the night sky, the comet rises and sets with the stars.

Sometime

But if you look carefully, each night you will see that the comet has moved. After a few weeks or months, it's gone.

You will be able to see comets better if you use binoculars. It also helps to go far away from city lights because the sky is darker in the country.

Sometime later

Comet Morehouse

Comet West

Palomar Observatory

We get some of our best views of comets through telescopes. Scientists called astronomers use large telescopes to study comets and other objects in the sky.

Skylab

Comet Ikeya-Seki

Comet Arend-Roland

Some comets have been observed by astronauts in orbit around the earth and by robot probes in space.

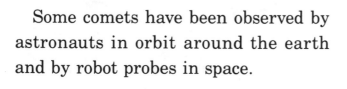

Kitt Peak National Observatory

Hundreds of years ago, before there were space probes, astronauts, or telescopes, people sometimes said comets were hairy stars. They thought the tails looked like long locks of hair or like beards.

German drawing of Halley's Comet from A.D. 684

Danish drawing of a comet from 1687

German drawing of a comet from 1661

Drawing of a comet from 1744

Of course, a comet is not really hairy, and it is not a star. Stars, like our distant, fiery sun, shine with their own light. The comet and its tail seem to glow like a flame, but the comet is not on fire. Most of the comet's light is reflected sunlight. The comet itself is so cold that your hand would freeze in the middle of it.

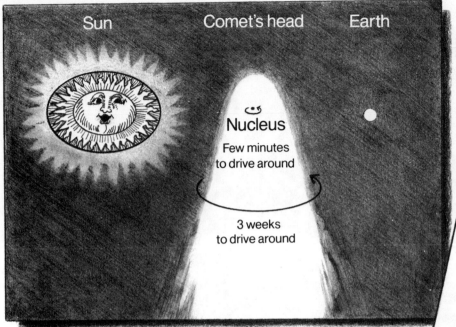

The comet's icy nucleus is about the size of a small mountain, but the gassy head of a comet is usually bigger than the whole earth. Some comet heads are even larger than the sun. If you could drive a car around a comet nucleus, you would make the trip in a few minutes. But it would take you three weeks of nonstop driving to go all the way around a comet's head.

The tail of gas and dust that sweeps away from a comet's head is millions of miles long. In 1910, the tail of Halley's Comet got long enough to stretch from the earth to the sun. That's about 93 million (93,000,000) miles. This tail was so long, it could have been wrapped around the earth almost 4,000 times.

Sun

Earth

93 million miles

Halley's Comet in 1910

Even though the comet is so big, there is hardly anything to it. A comet is mostly empty space. The air you breathe is millions of times thicker than most of the comet. A comet is the nearest thing to nothing that anything can be and still be something.

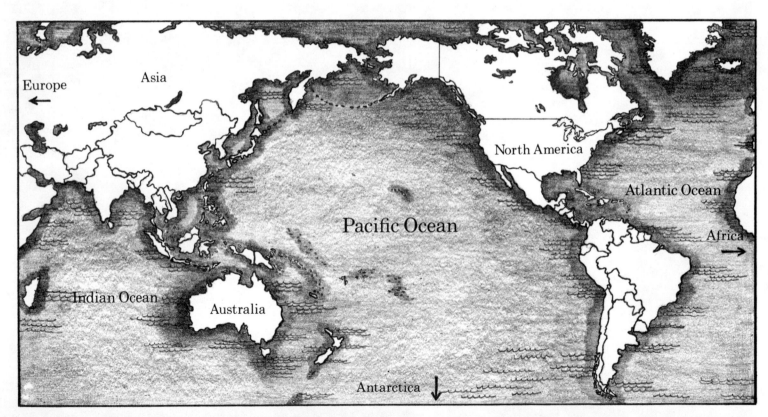

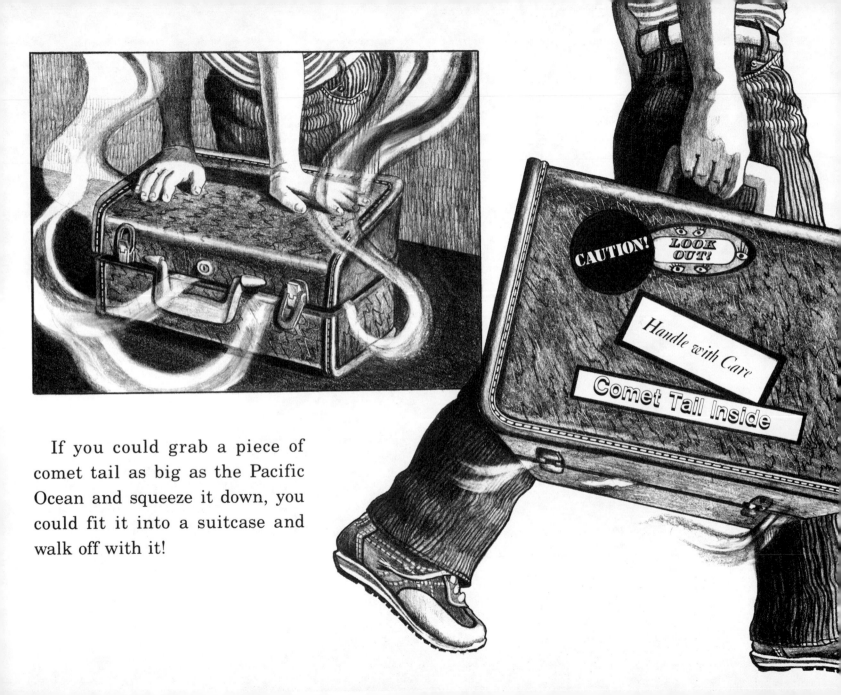

If you could grab a piece of comet tail as big as the Pacific Ocean and squeeze it down, you could fit it into a suitcase and walk off with it!

Most of the time comets don't even have tails. But once a comet gets close to the sun, the sun boils off some of it and blows it away into a tail. A comet's tail always points away from the sun. There is a wind blowing from the sun, and even sunlight pushes on the comet's tail. The tail is like a flag that

Your hair is like a comet's tail when the wind blows it. When you face the wind, your hair blows backward. With your back to the wind, your hair blows forward. If the wind blows hard enough, you can lose your hat.

This means that some of the comet escapes every time the comet rounds the sun. After going by the sun many times, most of the comet will be gone. Comets last a long time, but they don't last forever.

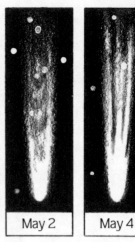

| April 26 | April 27 | April 30 | May 2 | May 4 | May 6 |

Halley's Comet in 1910

Did your great-grandparents see Halley's Comet in 1910? The President of the United States then was William Howard Taft. People drove Ford Model T automobiles, but they didn't have television, radio programs, or video games. Plastic wasn't used much, and toy cars were made out of metal. Horse-drawn wagons delivered milk to your door, and women almost always wore long dresses. How old will you be when Halley's Comet returns?

May 15 | May 23 | May 28 | June 3 | June 9 | June 11

William Howard Taft

1910

Nothing happened! There is practically nothing in a comet's tail. You can see stars right through it.

Still, there is something solid in the middle of all that nothing. There is a snowball as big as a city in the comet's head. Could one of these ever hit the earth?

It doesn't happen often, but it can happen. We think a piece of Encke's Comet may have been what hit Siberia in 1908. It was the size of a football field, and it devastated the landscape for 20 miles in every direction. If you had been sitting on a porch 55 miles from where it hit, you still would have been knocked over and knocked out.

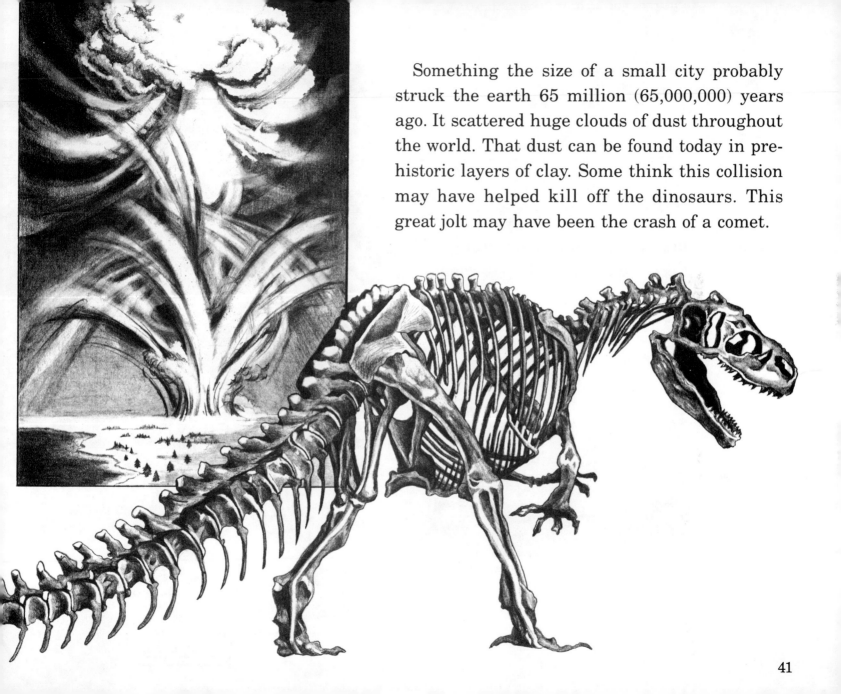

Something the size of a small city probably struck the earth 65 million (65,000,000) years ago. It scattered huge clouds of dust throughout the world. That dust can be found today in prehistoric layers of clay. Some think this collision may have helped kill off the dinosaurs. This great jolt may have been the crash of a comet.

If you had lived in ancient times, you would have been afraid of comets, but not because comets hit the earth. Collisions with comets are very rare. In those days, people thought comets might be dangerous, because they could never be sure when one might appear. Comets weren't like the sun, moon, planets, and stars. All of those were well behaved. But comets showed up by surprise.

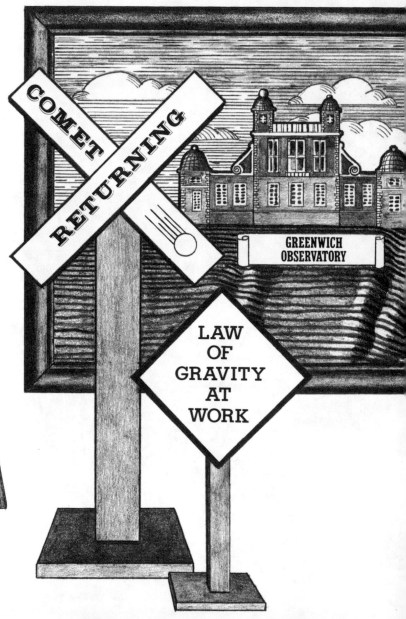

GREENWICH OBSERVATORY

COMET RETURNING

LAW OF GRAVITY AT WORK

EDMOND HALLEY AND ISAAC NEWTON IDEA COMPANY

Isaac Newton
Born 1642   Died 1727

Edmond Halley
Born 1656   Died 1742

In 1705, however, an English astronomer named Edmond Halley used Isaac Newton's law of gravity to predict—for the first time—a comet's return.

Edmond Halley was the Astronomer Royal of England and headquartered at Greenwich Observatory. He was born in 1656, died in 1742, and lived at about the same time as Isaac Newton. They knew each other well. Isaac Newton was the scientist who discovered that the force of gravity is what makes the planets follow their orbits around the sun.

Using this law of gravity, Halley figured out that a comet he had seen in 1682 would come back in 1758. And it did. This proved that comets are part of our solar system, too.

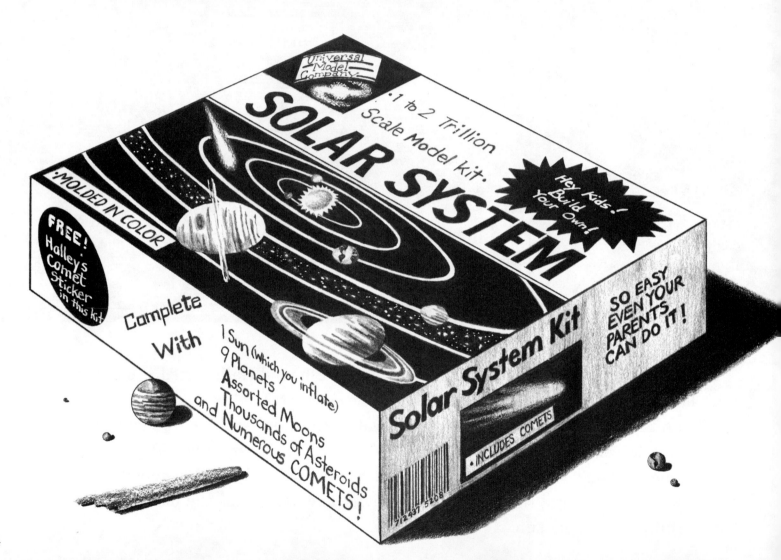

Edmond Halley didn't live to see his comet return, but we know that the same comet has been seen many times before. The Normans in France saw it in A.D. 1066, before they invaded England. They embroidered a scene with the comet into the Bayeux Tapestry.

Julius Caesar, a Roman general, saw it in 87 B.C., when he was about 13 years old. That was more than 2,000 years ago. Chinese astronomers may have seen the comet even before that, in 240 B.C. Their records mention a comet in that year.

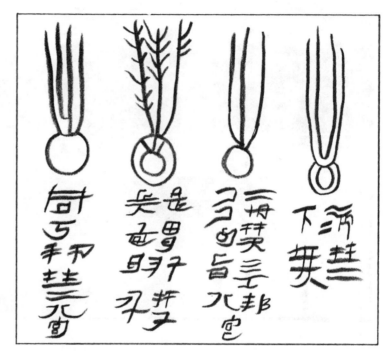

Because Edmond Halley predicted the comet would come back, it is now named after him. Today, most comets are named after the people who discover them. There are probably a lot more comets to be discovered. We think now that there is a great cloud of comets that travel around the sun.

This means you might find a comet. You'll have to look all over the sky, with a telescope, night after night, to be the first to see a new comet. But if you do, someday other people will watch a comet named after you.